Born to Swing

Lil Hardin Armstrong's Life in Jazz

MARA ROCKLIFF

ILLUSTRATED BY
MICHELE WOOD

CALKINS CREEK
AN IMPRINT OF HIGHLIGHTS
Honesdale, Pennsylvania

I was just born to swing, that's all. Call it what you want, blues, swing, jazz, it caught hold of me way back in Memphis and it looks like it won't ever let go.

—Lil Hardin Armstrong

I was born to swing, and that's the truth.

We lived in a boarding house in Memphis, just a little way from Beale Street, where the music never stopped.

The Father of the Blues himself, Mister W. C. Handy, used to march his band right down that street, and all the children would come running—but not me.

Oh, no. "Devil's music," my mother called it, and she kept me far away.

She couldn't keep me from the organ in the parlor, though. Every chance I got, I hopped up on that stool. My legs weren't long enough to reach the pedals, so I sent my little cousin crawling down below while I tickled the keys.

The day came I was good enough to play the organ at Sunday school. I'd play a hymn, but I would play it with a *beat*. The pastor used to frown at me over his spectacles, like this. Oh, I was swinging! I put something new in those old hymns. I didn't know it yet, but it was jazz.

I took piano lessons at Mrs. Hicks's School of Music. Her top student was a girl named Bertha, but I made up my mind that I'd be number one.

It came down to a contest, Bertha against me. I sat down at the piano and I flung myself into that music. Oh, boy. I flung myself so hard, I lost my place!

Now what? I had lost my place, but I was not about to lose that contest—not without a fight. I sat up straight and smiled, and I played that song right to the end. Well, I played *something*, anyway. Whatever came into my head and out my fingertips, that's what I played.

Later I would learn to call that "jamming." Improvising— that's what jazz musicians do. Back there at Mrs. Hicks's School of Music, nobody knew *what* to call it. But we all knew who the winner of that contest was.

My mother took pride in my talent, so long as I played the classics—Beethoven and Bach. Then one day, she caught me hiding Mister W. C. Handy's song "St. Louis Blues." She chased me with a broom, but it was too late. That new rhythm had already swept me off my feet.

Suddenly it seemed like everyone was on the move—
heading for the cities, heading north, for better opportunities.
The Great Migration had begun, and we went, too.

Chicago!

State Street was like Beale Street, only better. They called it the Stroll. I called it heaven. City lights, sharp dressers, music any hour of the day or night.

I was nearly grown, but I still looked just like a little girl. Eighty-five pounds, that's it. Nothing to show the city but the widest smile and the biggest, brightest eyes.

Out on the Stroll, I stopped to look into the window of a music store. All that sheet music. Oh, gee! How I wished I had the money to buy every song.

Inside, I asked if I could try a number out on their piano.

Mrs. Jones, the owner of the store, came over to hear me play. Next thing I knew, I had a job!

Every afternoon, I sat at that little piano by the window. Soon I'd learned all the latest songs. The store was packed with customers. They called me the Jazz Wonder Child.

One day, a man I'd never seen walked in the store. He sat down at that piano and—oh, boy! He had it rocking in no time at all. His feet were stomping. He played *hard*.

Everyone was jumping, going wild, calling out, "Oh, Jelly!" That was how I met the great Jelly Roll Morton, who invented jazz . . . or so he liked to say.

All the jazz musicians came into that music store to jam.
When a band needed a new musician, they called the store,
and Mrs. Jones would send somebody over to try out.

The New Orleans Creole Jazz Band needed a piano player.
But every man that Mrs. Jones sent over, they sent back. Finally,
she sent *me*.

A girl playing piano in a jazz band? Not in those days!
Women were "canaries"—singers. The musicians were all men.

I had to show them I was no canary. When the music started,
I hit those keys *hard*, like Jelly. I may have only weighed
eighty-five pounds, but I used every pound!

Did they send me back? What do you think?

There I was, swinging with the swingingest band in Chicago. I laid those rhythms down so hot, they called me Hot Miss Lil.

I was playing at the Dreamland when a fellow from New Orleans came to town—Louis Armstrong.

Louis was not a handsome man. His clothes were out of style. But when he blew that horn, oh, gee!

Soon we started walking out together. We'd play with the band all night, then hit the Stroll. Everybody in Chicago knew Miss Lil, and I made sure they all knew Louis Armstrong, too.

Naturally, we had a jazz wedding. Then we joined the band on tour. Every night, a different city. Every day, back on the road. It was no honeymoon! But we had each other, and we had our music. That was the Jazz Age. Seemed like all America was young and happy, just like us.

Louis and I wrote songs together, played together, even put a little band together to make records—the Hot Five. Oh, we were hot, all right. The sweat poured off us while we played our music into that recording horn. We played *hard*.

We thought the good times would last forever. But the Roaring Twenties ended with a crash. Hard times for America— and me. Louis was moving on.

Jazz moved on, too, and I moved right on with it. These were the days of the Big Bands. Duke Ellington, Cab Calloway— and me, Miss Lil. I did it all. I wrote the songs. I led the bands. Men, women—oh, it made no difference to me, so long as they could swing those tunes.

After the war, I tried out other things—
running a restaurant, designing clothes—but
the music wouldn't let me go.

It took me all the way to Paris, where the
French had flipped for *le jazz hot*.

Back home, everyone was going wild over a new kind of music they called "rock and roll." They'd forgotten about jazz, and me—or so I thought.

All those years making our music? Turned out we were making history.

The day came when people played my songs again. They put me on TV. They said I was a "living legend."

Miss Lil and jazz, we had grown up together and grown old together, but I never lost the beat.

You won't believe me, but I died at the piano, playing that "St. Louis Blues"—playing *hard*. Oh, boy! I went out swinging. Right up to the end, I had the widest smile and the biggest, brightest eyes.

"Hot Miss Lil" Hardin

Now, some folks got plenty money.
Some folks got philosophy.
But I've got good old swing,
And it's good enough for me!

—Lil Hardin Armstrong, "Born to Swing"

About Lil

Jazz pioneer Lillian Hardin Armstrong was a remarkable woman. At a time when only men played music professionally, wrote hit songs, ran recording sessions, or led their own bands, Lil did all those things and more.

Lil was born in 1898 in Memphis, Tennessee. As a young girl, she played organ and piano. She was trained as a classical musician; in her teens, she even studied music at Fisk University. But when she found jazz, she was hooked.

From her first job in her late teens, Lil quickly became a fixture of the Chicago jazz scene. She played with the New Orleans Creole Jazz Band (later King Oliver's) and other top bands, then went on to headline with her own band at Chicago's hottest black-owned club, the Dreamland Café. She organized groups of musicians to record under different names, including the Hot Five, Lil's Hot Shots, the New Orleans Wanderers, and the Hot Seven. She also composed and copyrighted songs, having her first hit with "Sweet Lovin' Man" in 1923.

Today, Lil is remembered for her famous husband, Louis Armstrong. But she was already well known before they met, and after they married, she used her reputation to boost his career. In 1925, the *Chicago Defender* asked, "Louis Armstrong. Who is he? . . . Louis is the feature man in Lil's jazz band at the Dreamland." No last name needed—in Chicago, just "Lil" was enough. Everybody knew whom the reporter meant.

In the 1930s, Lil worked as the house pianist for Decca Records while writing and recording many popular songs of her own, such as "Born to Swing," "Just for a Thrill," and "Brown Gal," which Ringo Starr of the Beatles would later record (with slightly different lyrics) as "Bad Boy." She led several big bands, including the all-female Harlem Harlicans.

After World War II, big bands declined in popularity, and Lil tried different kinds of work. She designed clothing—Louis Armstrong, now divorced from her but still on friendly terms, happily wore her suits onstage—and opened a restaurant, Lil Armstrong's Swing Shack, featuring dishes with jazz-themed names like Jam Session Pies and Boogie-Woogie Stew.

But Lil couldn't stay away from playing music for long. After a European tour in the 1950s, she enjoyed a comeback in the United States in the early 1960s, when there was a resurgence of interest in the early days of Chicago jazz.

Lil worked with many of the greatest jazz musicians of her time. They liked and accepted her and spoke about her with respect.

Saxophonist George Clarke:
She didn't dwell on any setbacks or adversity. She just went from one thing to another immediately, and with new vigor and new vim and great enthusiasm.

Singer Alberta Hunter:
She could play anything in this world. . . . She was marvelous.

Trombonist Preston Jackson:
Man, Lil didn't know how much she could swing.

Listen to Lil

Many of Lil Hardin Armstrong's songs can be found online. You might try starting with these. As Lil would say, "Just listen and be sent."

"Chimes Blues." King Oliver's Creole Jazz Band, 1923.

"My Heart." Louis Armstrong and His Hot Five, 1925.

"Perdido Street Blues." New Orleans Wanderers, 1926.

"Brown Gal." Lil Hardin Armstrong and Her Swing Orchestra, 1936.

"Just for a Thrill." Lil Hardin Armstrong and Her Swing Orchestra, 1936.

"Born to Swing." Lil Hardin Armstrong and Her Swing Orchestra, 1937.

"Eastown Boogie." Lil Hardin Armstrong and Her Orchestra, 1961.

Lil with King Oliver's Creole Jazz Band in 1923. Future husband Louis Armstrong kneels beside her, jokingly posing with a trombone instead of his cornet.

Timeline

1898   Lil Hardin is born February 3 in Memphis, Tennessee.

1914   W. C. Handy publishes "St. Louis Blues."

1914–1918   World War I and the beginning of the Great Migration, in which six million African Americans move from the rural South to cities in the North, Midwest, and West.

1918   Lil moves to Chicago, Illinois, with her family.

1924   Lil marries Louis Armstrong.

1925–1926   Lil organizes the groundbreaking Hot Five recording sessions, for which she composes many songs, including "My Heart" and "Lonesome Blues."

1929   Stock market crash ends the Roaring Twenties, sets off the Great Depression.

1936   Lil records her classic song "Just for a Thrill," later sung by many others, including singers Ray Charles and Aretha Franklin.

1938   After many years apart, Lil and Louis finally divorce; she will never marry again.

1939–1945   World War II.

1952   Lil tours Europe; in Paris, she records an album with jazz saxophonist Sidney Bechet.

1950s   Rock and roll music storms the pop charts.

1961	Riverside Records releases *Chicago: The Living Legends: Lil Hardin Armstrong and Her Orchestra.*
	Lil appears on NBC television special "Chicago and All That Jazz."
1971	Lil dies in Chicago August 27 while playing at a televised memorial concert for her recently deceased ex-husband, Louis.

Author's Note

Lil Hardin Armstrong didn't write this book, of course. But in a way, she did.

When she died (and yes, she really did die at the piano, playing the song that had once made her mother chase her with a broom), Lil was working on a book about her life. But that book was never published. It just disappeared.

Since Lil never got to tell her own story, I tried to tell it as she might have chosen to. I used many of her own words from the interviews she gave over the years. Like all stories told aloud, Lil's stories changed a little every time she told them. Sometimes she even bent the truth a bit. Reading what other people said about her helped me bend it back.

—MR

Bibliography

All quotations used in the book can be found in the following sources marked with an asterisk(*).

PRIMARY SOURCES

"Jones Music Store, Jelly Roll, and Handsome Men . . . ," "The New Orleans Creole Jazz Band," and other extracts from early draft of Lil Hardin Armstrong's unpublished memoir, co-written with journalist Chris Albertson, posted by Chris Albertson at stomp-off.blogspot.com in 2009.

*"Lil Armstrong." *Down Beat*, June 1, 1951. "Louis Armstrong" and "Preston Jackson," also from *Down Beat* (dates unknown). Interviews excerpted in *Hear Me Talkin' to Ya: The Story of Jazz by the Men Who Made It*, edited by Nat Shapiro and Nat Hentoff. New York: Rinehart, 1955, pp. 80, 91–95, 95–96, 101, 102, 104, 115, 206.

"Lil Armstrong, 1957." Interview in *And They All Sang: Adventures of an Eclectic Disc Jockey* by Studs Terkel. New York: New Press, 2005, pp. 139–144.

"Lil Hardin Armstrong." Transcript of oral history recorded in New Orleans, January 19, 1969. Williams Research Center, Historic New Orleans Collection, New Orleans, Louisiana.

"Lillian Hardin Armstrong." Transcript of oral history recorded in Chicago, July 1, 1959. Hogan Jazz Archive, Tulane University, New Orleans, Louisiana.

"Satchmo and Me: Lil Armstrong's Own Story." Interview, 1956. Riverside Jazz Archives Series, 12–120. Complete transcription in *American Music,* Spring 2007, pp. 106–118.

SECONDARY SOURCES

Bergreen, Laurence. *Louis Armstrong: An Extravagant Life*. New York: Broadway Books, 1997.

*Brothers, Thomas. *Louis Armstrong: Master of Modernism*. New York: W. W. Norton, 2014.

Dahl, Linda. *Stormy Weather: The Music and Lives of a Century of Jazzwomen*. New York: Limelight Editions, 1989.

*Dickerson, James L. *Just for a Thrill: Lil Hardin Armstrong, First Lady of Jazz*. New York: Cooper Square Press, 2002.

Handy, D. Antoinette. *Black Women in American Bands and Orchestras*. 2nd ed. Lanham, MD: Scarecrow Press, 1998.

Jones, Max, and John Chilton. *Louis: The Louis Armstrong Story, 1900–1971*. Boston: Little, Brown, 1971.

*Placksin, Sally. *American Women in Jazz, 1900 to the Present: Their Words, Lives, and Music*. New York: Wideview Books, 1982.

Teachout, Terry. *Pops: A Life of Louis Armstrong*. Boston: Houghton Mifflin Harcourt, 2009.

Picture Credits

Courtesy of the Driggs Collection at Jazz at Lincoln Center: 28, 30

Acknowledgments

Special thanks to the experts who generously took the time to correspond or speak with me: Bruce Raeburn, curator of the Hogan Jazz Archive at Tulane University; Sherrie Tucker, professor of American Studies at the University of Kansas; Chris Albertson, journalist; and Dan Morgenstern, director emeritus of the Institute of Jazz Studies at Rutgers University.

For Michael Rockliff, the best advance man a daughter could have —*MR*

To young artists whose voices of dedication, determination, and defying the odds lead them through journeys of success. How great thou ART! —*MW*

Calkins Creek · An Imprint of Highlights · 815 Church Street · Honesdale, Pennsylvania 18431 · Printed in China

ISBN: 978-1-62979-555-3 · Library of Congress Control Number: 2017942222 · First edition 10 9 8 7 6 5 4 3 2 1

Designed by Barbara Grzeslo
The text is set in Times New Roman. The illustrations are done in acrylic paint.